S0-BSD-741

Hector Guimard

F. LANIER GRAHAM

THE MUSEUM OF MODERN ART, NEW YORK

LIBRARY
COLBY-SAWYER COLLEGE
NEW LONDON, NH 03257

PHOTOGRAPH CREDITS

Courtesy of Architectural Record, New York: 17 left; Courtesy of Cooper-Hewitt Museum of Decorative Arts and Design, Smithsonian Institution, New York: 23 above; James Grady, Atlanta: 19 right; Laurent Sully Jaulmes, Paris: 7, 8, 9 right, 10 above, 10 below, 11, 13 below, 14 above, 14 below, 15, 17 right, 21, 23 below, 24, 25, 27, 29, 30, 31, 32 above, 33, 34, 37; Kunstgewerbemuseum, Zurich: 26; Musée des Arts Décoratifs, Paris: 18, 20; Stan Ries, New York: 8, 12, 13 above, 16, 28, 32 bottom; H. Roger Viollet, Paris: 19 left.

© Copyright 1970, The Museum of Modern Art
11 West 53 Street, New York, New York 10019
Library of Congress Catalogue Card Number 69-11451
Designed by Patricia Maka
Type set by Ruttle, Shaw & Wetherill, Inc.,
Philadelphia, Pa.
Printed by The Meriden Gravure Company,
Meriden, Conn.

 # 81368

cover: Wallpaper. 1896

NA
1053
.G8
G7
c.1

SCHEDULE OF THE EXHIBITION

The Museum of Modern Art, New York
March 10–May 10, 1970

California Palace of the Legion of Honor, San Francisco
July 23–August 30, 1970

Art Gallery of Ontario, Toronto
September 25–November 9, 1970

Musée des Arts Décoratifs, Paris
January 15–April 11, 1971

LENDERS TO THE EXHIBITION

Mr. and Mrs. Alfred H. Barr, Jr., New York; Martin J. Eidelburg, New Brunswick, New Jersey; Barlach Heuer, Paris; John Jesse, London; Alastair B. Martin, New York; Lillian Nassau, New York; Laurent Oppenheim, Jr., New York; Parfums Revillon—F. Millot, Paris; Henri Poupée, Paris; Stan Ries, New York; Gerhard P. Woeckel, Munich.

Association d'Étude et de Défense de l'Architecture et des Arts Décoratifs du XXe Siècle, Garches; Museum für Kunst und Gewerbe, Hamburg; Cooper-Hewitt Museum of Decorative Arts and Design, Smithsonian Institution, New York; The Metropolitan Museum of Art, New York; The Museum of Modern Art, New York; Archives de Paris; Bibliothèque Forney, Paris; Bibliothèque des Arts Décoratifs, Paris; Musée des Arts Décoratifs, Paris; Musée d'Art Moderne de la Ville de Paris; Philadelphia Museum of Art.

ACKNOWLEDGMENTS

An exhibition of this scope, with so many of Guimard's most important works, would not have been possible without the sponsorship of the Ministère des Affaires Étrangères of the French Republic, and the Association Française d'Action Artistique, which has underwritten the transportation and insurance of the French loans; the close collaboration of the Musée des Arts Décoratifs, which has been responsible for assembling the French loans; and the cooperation of the numerous lenders themselves, whose names are listed above. On behalf of the Trustees of The Museum of Modern Art and of the participating museums, I wish to express sincere appreciation for their generosity.

During the preparations for this exhibition, which began in 1965, and for the critical study of Guimard's work, which will be published later this year, I have been fortunate to enjoy considerable assistance from many individuals. Gaston Diehl of the Ministère des Affaires Étrangères; Edouard Morot-Sir, formerly Cultural Counselor to His Excellency the Ambassador of France to the United States; François Mathey and particularly Yvonne Brunhammer of the Musée des Arts Décoratifs have been extremely helpful.

To Alain Blondel, Ralph Culpepper, Yves Plantin, and Stan Ries, who have collaborated with me on the forthcoming monograph and *catalogue raisonné*, my debt is immeasurable. Their tireless research into the details of the life and work of an artist about whom very little was previously known has provided the basis for the entire project. Gratitude also is owed, for their sensitive photography, Stan Ries and especially Laurent Sully Jaulmes, who provided almost all of the illustrations in this catalogue.

Limitations of space make it impossible to thank here all the individuals whose contributions will be acknowledged in the forthcoming book. But I am particularly grateful to Alfred H. Barr, Jr., for his encouragement at the inception of this undertaking; Arthur Drexler for allowing time away from regular responsibilities; Ludwig Glaeser and Mildred Constantine for curatorial assistance; Richard Palmer for solving innumerable administrative problems; Helen M. Franc for invaluable editorial suggestions; Harriet Schoenholz for sensitive editing; Patricia Maka for her sympathetic design; Eric B. Rowlison and Judy Walenta for skillful registration; Emily Fuller and Stuart Edelson not only for their secretarial and custodial assistance, but also for their good spirits.

F. L. G.

Hector Guimard (1867–1942) has been recognized as the most important French architect-designer in all the major surveys of Art Nouveau. However, this evaluation is based on very few examples of his work. His only famous monument is the system of subway entrances designed for the Paris Métro company in 1900. These entrances, many of which are still standing, are so distinctive a synthesis of Art Nouveau qualities that the entire movement was popularly referred to at the time as "Style Métro." Besides that series of designs, even specialists are familiar with little more than three or four buildings, and one or two suites of furniture. Guimard's contemporary reputation as the Parisian "Pontiff" of Art Nouveau was based on considerably more. Recent research has uncovered more than fifty buildings executed between about 1890 and 1930, hundreds of decorative objects, and over two thousand drawings. Although there remain many gaps in our knowledge, it is finally possible to view Guimard's work as a whole.

In 1885 Guimard entered the Paris École des Beaux-Arts where he was encouraged by the principles of Eugène-Emmanuel Viollet-le-Duc and other Rationalists to study the past, not in order to imitate it, but to make use of it in the development of an entirely new style. This departure from the accepted tradition of creative copying was so radical that Guimard's fellow students compared him with a notorious political anarchist named Ravachol who was bombing churches at the time, and dubbed him the "Ravachol of architecture."

Guimard began his practice in 1888. Convinced that the eclectic works around him were "cold receptacles of various past styles in which the original spirit was no longer alive enough to dwell," and that every aspect of architecture and design must "bear as proudly as an heraldic crest, the mark of contemporary art," he undertook his *recherche d'un style nouveau.* His first houses of the early 1890s, for which he drew upon the most progressive structural and ornamental aspects of the Neo-Gothic tradition, were exhibited as *maisons modernes.* By 1893 he had created his first Early Art Nouveau de-

signs, which seem to be the earliest known examples in French architecture. His independent activity was confirmed by an interview with Victor Horta in the summer of 1895, when they discussed the advantages of abandoning "the leaf and the flower, retaining only the stem." Catalyzed by Horta's rationale of abstract linearity, Guimard continued to develop his new style of ornament with revolutionary fervor during the outfitting of the Castel Béranger apartment house.

The animating idea behind Guimard's High Art Nouveau style may be described as "abstract naturalism." His aim was not an illustration of the appearance of nature, but an abstraction of its fundamental processes. Holding up his cane (page 30) as an example, Guimard once used the analogy of sap running through trees to communicate his abstract idea. He said that the flowing of sap through trees is an essential characteristic, like the qualities he wanted to represent in his art, not something like the flowing of sap in particular, but the "sap of things" in general. The best-known examples of his "abstract naturalism" are the structural "stalks" of the Métro (pages 14, 15) and the Humbert de Romans Concert Hall (pages 16, 17). But the abstract rendering in naturalistic form of the intrinsic properties of whatever material he was dealing with typifies all his work after about 1896.

An indication of the precise manner in which Guimard approached nature survives in a report written by the distinguished critic, Gustave Soulier, in close collaboration with Guimard. The following excerpt refers to a design for *papier-mâché* wainscoting (page 28): ". . . we do not see . . . clearly recognizable motifs which are only interpreted and regularized by a geometric ornamental convention. But neither is it merely withered and graceless floral or animal skeletons that Mr. Guimard draws. He is inspired by the underlying movements, by the creative process in nature that reveals to us identical formulas through its numerous manifestations. And he assimilates these principles in the formation of his ornamental contours. . . . [Thus] the floret is not an exact representation of any particular flower. Here is an art that both abbreviates and amplifies the immediate facts of Nature; it spiritualizes them. We are present at the birth of the quintessence of a flower." (*Études sur le Castel Béranger*, 1899)

By the mid 1890s Guimard was convinced it was his duty as an architect to preside over the design and execution of every detail of his buildings. Toward that end, he apprenticed himself to every type of structural and decorative craft. As he subordinated his formal impulse to techniques of fabrication, his animated sense of objectivity gave a fresh reality to his material. He articulated his material so that the animus that he had projected into it could be empathetically perceived. The rationale for his approach to the "nature" of wrought iron is characteristic: ". . . in the iron foundry, is it logical to give a calm form to the iron stalks which carry weight, and consequently exert effort? Also is it right to model flowers, ribbons, or fruits with this iron? Guimard did not think so; he believed it was more logical to preserve in the iron its slender rigidity and its nervous suppleness; he preferred that iron retain its ironness. And let anyone say he was wrong while looking at the gate of Castel Béranger." (Gustave Soulier, *Études sur le Castel Béranger*, 1899)

Before Castel Béranger, individual decorative specialties had been "modernized" by artists such as Émile Gallé and Victor Prouvé. But no one in France, before or after Castel Béranger, approached every kind of domestic design problem with contemporary sensibility. Within each subdivision of the decorative arts, Guimard has left a body of work that normally would be enough to insure an enduring reputation for a specialized artisan. Throughout all of Art Nouveau, perhaps only Henry van de Velde, who was also a painter, worked as successfully in more media.

With the outfitting of this one apartment house, Guimard came close to achieving the first of his stated ambitions—the total modernization of French decorative arts. He was proud of his achievement as a *maître d'oeuvre*, and in 1898 produced a lavish portfolio of hand-colored plates illustrating every brick and bolt and branch that had been the object of his meditation. Assisted by a large publicity campaign, supervised by Guimard himself, the influence of the building and the book was enormous. The difference between the Early Art Nouveau decoration in the France of 1895, when ideas from around the world were still being assimilated, and the mature High Art Nouveau decoration that France exhibited at the Paris Exposition of 1900 owes a fundamental debt to Guimard.

Guimard was hardly content with having "modernized" the decorative arts. He wanted to expand the formal principles he had developed in his architectural decoration to encompass his architectural construction. This widening of focus is reflected in his ego image; by 1899 he had begun to sign his work "Hector Guimard, Architecte d'Art."

The long chronology of Castel Béranger made it inevitable that its architecture of 1894–95, and its outfitting of about 1896–99, would be stylistically inconsistent—the flowering of Art Nouveau decoration on Neo-Gothic construction. But in a brilliant series of buildings between 1898 and 1901 Guimard achieved his ultimate ambition of creating complete works of art, which were entirely original, formal unities. The major monuments of this short period, in which he designed and personally supervised the construction of at least ten projects other than the Métro, include the Coilliot House in Lille, Castel Henriette in Sèvres, and the Humbert de Romans Concert Hall in Paris. In all these buildings, the stylistic traits that had enlivened the nonarchitectural aspects of Castel Béranger became primary characteristics of both the exterior and interior design. Gradually, first in elevation and then in plan, the whole of his architecture and decoration became totally integrated environments.

Soon after the Paris Exposition of 1900, Art Nouveau began to lose its short-lived popularity. Increasingly isolated by fewer commissions, Guimard began to differentiate himself from other practitioners and imitators of Art Nouveau by insisting that his work be identified as "Style Guimard." Again his idea of himself corresponded with a stylistic change, a refinement of the Art Nouveau style, which lasted from about 1901–2, to about 1910–12.

During this "Style Guimard" period the exuberance of his earlier years gradually became more restrained. He was no longer questioning with an intense series of extraordinary experiments the assumptions history had handed down about what a house or a chair should look like. By this time he had formed his own fundamental principles. Confident of their validity, he proceeded to refine them with a more controlled vibrance.

As is clear from the difference between the furniture for Castel Béranger (pages 8, 9) and Nozal House (pages 18, 20, 26), the spatial disparities disappear. Transitional intervals, once distinctly dissident, become smoothly polished. Attention shifts from raw, undecorated linearity to highly plastic volumes of space enriched by "civilizing" ornament. Hard, dark mahogany is replaced by soft, blond pearwood. Symmetry eventually replaces asymmetry. Although the flow of energy was under tighter discipline, his imagination was no less productive. Long

5

after most of his colleagues had abandoned Art Nouveau, Guimard continued to produce work of surprising originality such as Guimard House (pages 22, 23) and the interior of Mezzara House (pages 24, 25).

Several years before World War I another stylistic transition began from "Style Guimard" to the Art Moderne or Art Déco style, which he continued to use throughout the 1920s for a series of apartment houses and with which he completed his career. Even in the mid-1920s decorative elements of his prewar style remained an integral part of his compositions, making Guimard both the first and the last Art Nouveau architect in France.

During these two decades, another generation of progressive architects, freed from eclecticism by Art Nouveau, was attempting to achieve another kind of architecture and design. These efforts, culminating in the practices of the Bauhaus, employed wholeheartedly those industrial techniques of greater social utility with which Guimard had only begun to experiment. The romanticism of the machine replaced the romanticism of nature as the muse of architecture and design.

In 1925 Guimard, as an elder statesman of the old school, was uncertain as to the lasting value of machine-inspired art. "Today's Fashion of the Naked," he said, "corresponds to a whole state of mind: we no longer believe in mystery." But he was positive enough to hope that for the simplicity appropriate to mass production there would be found a set of formal ideals as basic and enduring as his own naturalistic aesthetic. Guimard himself was not able to contribute a great deal to these efforts, even though he experimented with industrial design and prefabricated architecture. His particular brilliance belonged to an age of spontaneity.

In evaluating Guimard's work, there are certain difficulties in isolating its various aspects. Rarely did he design a building without also outfitting it with individual solutions for every exterior and interior detail. And seldom did he design a decorative object outside of a specific architectural context. Whether one singles out his designs for buildings, furniture, wallpaper, or doorknobs; whether one discusses his treatment of space, mass, light, volume, color, texture, or line; whether one considers him as an architect, planner, craftsman, draftsman, graphic designer, industrial designer, jeweler, or sculptor; more often than not, these aspects are only partial components of a single, comprehensive aesthetic.

The desire for a *Gesamtkunst*—a total work of art—was widespread throughout Art Nouveau. But in the many attempts at such an ideal, the quality of the architecture and design were of equal interest in the work of only a few architect-designers. For comparisons appropriate to Guimard's distinctive achievements there are no parallels in France. One must look to such figures as Victor Horta in Belgium, Antoni Gaudí in Spain, Charles Rennie Mackintosh in Scotland, and Frank Lloyd Wright in the United States.

The totality of his concern for the quality of life, and the humanity of his planning with a new style for a new age, are only part of Guimard's relevance to our own time. The less obvious value of his formal contributions has lain dormant during the rise of machine-age aesthetics. As a lyric poet, his approach to design problems was not so straightforward as the more muscular prose of his better known contemporaries, whose formal vocabularies anticipated more directly the geometrically oriented compositions of economically superior production techniques.

The fact that in his ornament Guimard posed and resolved fundamental questions of nonfigurative abstraction a decade before that idea entered the mainstream of modern art is more a part of the history of painting and sculpture than the history of architecture and design. It is significant that Guimard's work received a far greater response from Dali and Picasso, for example, than from Le Corbusier. The manner in which Guimard was able to represent natural processes rather than illustrate natural appearances is suggestive of Surrealism; his *"art du geste"* anticipates Abstract Expressionism.

Nevertheless, modern architects have never entirely lost interest in the kind of compositional ideal Guimard's work represents. The same dream of formal freedom preoccupied a number of important figures, from Eric Mendelsohn, Rudolf Steiner, and Hermann Finsterlin in the 1920s, before the Bauhaus systematized its aesthetics, to Le Corbusier, Eero Saarinen, and Frederick Kiesler in the 1950s, when the influence of the Bauhaus began to loosen its grip on the avant-garde. But the search for fluid form has been severely restricted by technical and economic considerations. There are indications that some of these limitations may be disappearing. Houses are being made out of a thin cement mix sprayed over elastic webbings, urethane foam sprayed over balloons, and furniture simply poured.

Ultimately the value of Guimard's work is its own quality, which is all the more outstanding for having been realized with materials and spatial conceptions that had to be coaxed out of traditional configurations. What is relevant to the most advanced technical investigations of today is Guimard's unrestrained sense of form. He came very close to treating materials and spaces as amorphous lumps of clay. With such sculptural freedom, the only limitation is one's imagination.

CATALOGUE OF THE EXHIBITION

The following list includes all projects represented in the exhibition, whether by photographs or by original works; only the actual objects, drawings, and prints are numbered. According to the manner in which the exhibition is installed, the catalogue is divided into two parts. In the first part (pages 8–25) entries are listed chronologically according to the building for which they were designed or that to which they are most closely related stylistically. In the second part (pages 26–35) entries are listed chronologically within groupings of design categories.

The dates given for each building indicate the time between the beginning of design and the completion of construction, followed by the year in which outfitting was completed. For individual items, many of which were used for more than one building, the date indicates the year in which the design was first used. A date is enclosed in parentheses when it does not appear on the work. Dimensions are given in feet and inches, height preceding width. An asterisk indicates that the piece was available for presentation in New York only.

The abbreviation A.E.D.A.A.D.XX. indicates the Association d'Étude et de Défense de l'Architecture et des Arts Décoratifs du XXᵉ Siècle, in Garches, the archives of which contain hundreds of Guimard documents from the collection of M. Félix Brunau.

Castel Béranger, entrance. 1894–97

Guimard in his office, ca. 1900. (Postcard. 1903. Société Historique d'Auteuil et de Passy, Paris)

CASTEL BÉRANGER APARTMENT HOUSE
14–16 rue La Fontaine, Paris
1894–98; outfitting ca. 1899

Castel Béranger is Guimard's best-known building, although stylistic inconsistencies prevent it from being recognized as his masterpiece. Its architecture continues the dramatic structural emphasis, picturesque asymmetry, rich color, and elaborate ornamental impulse of the Neo-Gothic tradition, which characterize Guimard's early work, while the planning of the thirty-eight unique suites anticipates the spontaneity of his later style. Each major room and minor staircase is open to light from a street or courtyard; traditionally wasted space is filled with artists' studios and modest roof gardens. The originality of his scheme resulted in an exterior of unprecedented freedom, for which he received a Concours de Façades prize from the City of Paris in 1899.

While outfitting Castel Béranger, Guimard began to develop his own idea of the flowing processes of nature. The furniture from these early years provides the most dramatic examples of his naturalistic approach to the recalcitrant qualities of his materials. Rejecting the device of applied ornament, he used only the formal asymmetry associated with wood branching. Although Guimard designed the basic decoration for all the apartments, it was only his slightly later office suite that was outfitted entirely with furniture and accessories. Here one can sense the concept of the "total work of art" that was developing in his mind.

1. Test panel for vestibule. (1896–97). Enameled ceramic, 11⅝ x 24⅝″. Private collection, Paris

2. Study for couch. (1897). Pencil on tracing paper, 4⅝ x 7⅞″. A.E.D.A.A.D.XX.

3. Couch. (1897). Mahogany and tooled leather, 36½ x 67½″. The Museum of Modern Art, New York. Gift of Phyllis B. Lambert, 1964

4. Couch with overhead cabinet. (1897). Mahogany without original upholstery, 8′4⅜″ x 7′6¾″. Private collection, Paris. *Page 9*

5. Study for fireplace and frame. (1897–98). Green ink on tracing paper, 14¼ x 12¼″. A.E.D.A.A.D.XX.

6. Fireplace. (1897–98). Cast iron with enameled lava panels, 50 x 68¼″. Barlach Heuer, Paris

7. Study for a vase stand. 1899. Crayon, pastel, and pencil on tracing paper, 15½ x 14⅞″. A.E.D.A.A.D.XX.

8. Studies for a vase stand. (1899). Crayon, pastel, and pencil on tracing paper, 23 x 27⅝″. A.E.D.A.A.D.XX.

9. Vase stand. (ca. 1899). Ebony, 57½″ high. Museum für Kunst und Gewerbe, Hamburg. Purchase, 1900.*

10. Desk. (ca. 1899; remodeled after 1909). Olive wood with ash panels, 29¾″ x 8′4½″. The Museum of Modern Art, New York. Gift of Madame Hector Guimard, 1949. *Page 9*

Desk. ca. 1899

Couch with overhead cabinet. 1897

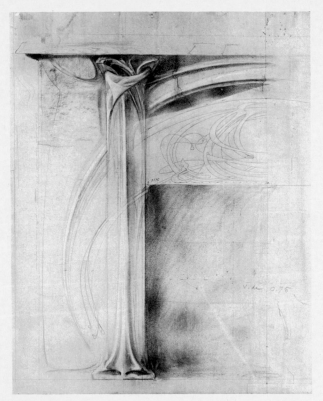

Study for fireplace. 1903

COILLIOT HOUSE AND STORE
14 rue de Fleurs, Lille
1898–1900; outfitting 1903

The Lille house is one of the first buildings in which Guimard unified an interior and exterior in the mature Art Nouveau style. This combination store and house for a ceramics contractor is faced with vivid green enameled lava blocks that dramatically advertise the client's merchandise. Unlike most of Guimard's major buildings, almost every detail of its façade and vestibule survive intact, as do several pieces of furniture from the elegant second-floor apartment.

Although severely restricted by the site, which recedes diagonally from the street, the composition contains most of the traits that were to continue to characterize his architecture and design: a plan ordered with increasing freedom; a new kind of asymmetry now made dynamic by unresolved tensions; surfaces so responsive to modulations of design they seem to be invested with almost anatomical sensibility; and an interest in Gothic motifs, such as the pointed and rampant arches, which never entirely disappear from Guimard's vocabulary.

11. Wall frame. (ca. 1899–1901). Fruitwood, 28 x 29″. Private collection, Paris

12. Study for fireplace. (1903). Crayon, pastel, and pencil on paper, 46½ x 51″. A.E.D.A.A.D.XX. *Page 10*

Vestibule
opposite: Façade

CASTEL HENRIETTE
46 rue des Binelles, Sèvres
1899–1900; remodeled ca. 1903; demolished 1969

Castel Henriette represents the highest flight of Guimard's architectural imagination. Although a number of his previous houses had been highly chromatic and complicated, this *maison de plaisance* was kaleidoscopically rich. The characteristic of tense complexity did not begin to influence his architectural volumes until he built completely three-dimensional country houses on open sites, far from the physical and psychological restrictions of the city. At Castel Henriette, for the first time, all the elements of both plan and elevation are distributed with the same sense of spontaneous compression and release that had dominated his two-dimensional designs. It is almost as if the freely modeled volumes were projected into their positions by centrifugal force. The composition is a triumph of deliberate tensions.

13. Newel post. (ca. 1900). Fruitwood, 39⅜ x 3⅛″. Private collection, Paris. *Page 13*

14. Bathroom tile. (ca. 1900). Glass paste, 3¾ x 3¾″. Private collection, San Francisco

Detail of exterior

Detail of newel post. ca. 1900

opposite: Front perspective. (Postcard. ca. 1900. Private collection, San Francisco)

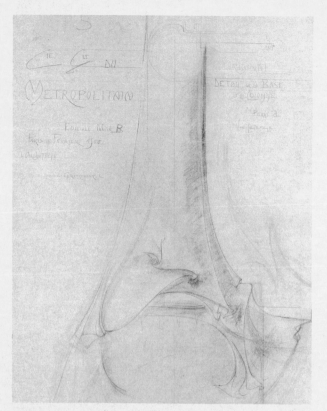

Study for base of archway. 1900

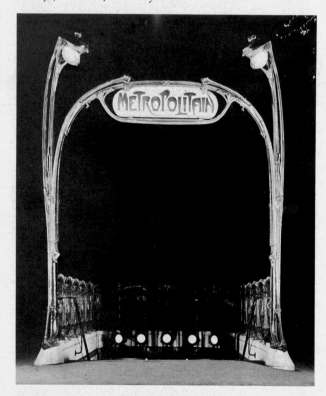

Entrance, Monceau Station. 1900

opposite: Covered entrance, Port Dauphine Station. 1900

MÉTROPOLITAIN ENTRANCE SYSTEM
Paris
Designed 1900; installed from 1900 to 1913

The system of subway entrances Guimard designed for the Métro company is the most famous project of his career. One hundred forty-one models were installed throughout the city between 1900 and 1913, of which ninety-one are still in use, seven having been classified as historical monuments. The design of this system is a vibrant example of Guimard's ability to combine the formal energy of his "abstract naturalism" with function. Contemporary critics and later writers have cited it as the quintessence of Art Nouveau. The Métro entrances were singularly responsible for publicizing the "New Art"—previously only familiar to an initiated few—by bringing the style to "every street corner." Public reaction ranged from the horror of established critics to the admiration of younger artists. Technically, the flexible modularity of the prefabricated components—cast iron, glass, and ceramic—designed to be used for many different kinds of sites and traffic situations, makes the Métro Guimard's most important contribution to the history of industrial design.

15. Study for base of archway. 1900. Crayon and pastel on paper, 41¾ x 28¾". A.E.D.A.A.D.XX. *Page 14*

16. Study for sign frame of archway. (1900). Crayon and pastel on paper, 35⅜ x 54". A.E.D.A.A.D.XX.

17. Archway from Raspail Station. (1900). Cast iron, painted green, 15'5" x 21'. The Museum of Modern Art, New York. Gift of Régie Autonome des Transports Parisiens, 1958.*

18. Study for railing panel. (1900). Crayon and pastel on tracing paper, 31⅜ x 23⅜". A.E.D.A.A.D.XX.

19. Panel for railing. (1900). Cast iron, painted green, 29½ x 24¾". The Museum of Modern Art, New York. Gift of Régie Autonome des Transports Parisiens, 1958

Interior of auditorium, ca. 1901. (Postcard. 1903. The Museum of Modern Art, New York)

HUMBERT DE ROMANS CONCERT HALL
60 rue Saint-Didier, Paris
1897–1901; demolished 1905

This concert hall, the largest in Paris at the time, is Guimard's most significant contribution to the history of architecture. Like Horta's *Maison du Peuple* of 1897–99, the auditorium may be ranked as one of the major achievements of Art Nouveau. One of the few critics who saw the interior before it was destroyed observed that the hall was: "formed of a visible structure, springing from the ground at each corner and spreading in graceful curves like the branches of an immense tree, in a way which gives somewhat the idea of a corner of a druidic forest. The main branches, eight in number, support a rather high cupola, pierced, like the sides, with bays filled with pale yellow stained-glass, through which an abundance of light finds its way into the hall. The framework is of steel, but the metal is covered with mahogany . . . the result is the most elaborate roof ever conceived by a French architect." (Fernand Mazade, *The Architectural Record*, 1902)

20. Plans and elevations. (1898). Black print, 11 x 17¼". The Museum of Modern Art, New York. Given anonymously, 1969

21. Study for plan of roof structure. (ca. 1898–99). Black and blue crayon and pencil on tracing paper, 29½ x 22¼". A.E.D.A.A.D.XX.

22. Longitudinal section. 1900. Sepia print and ink, 25⅜ x 38⅜". A.E.D.A.A.D.XX.

23. Transversal section. 1900. Sepia print, 26¾ x 38⅝". A.E.D.A.A.D.XX.

Detail of interior. (Photo ca. 1901)

Detail of pier. (Photo ca. 1901)

Bedroom suite. ca. 1904–7

NOZAL HOUSE

52 rue du Ranelagh, Paris
1902–5; outfitting ca. 1907; remodeled 1937; demolished 1958

In the preliminary plan for this palatial mansion a profusion of cells proliferates from the central core as freely and complexly as a living organism. As built, the scheme was somewhat restrained, owing to the more conservative wishes of Guimard's client. Nevertheless, the house was an extraordinary piece of sculpture. Only the slightly later work of Antoni Gaudí attained comparable qualities of fluid modulation in plan, elevation, and decoration.

Like the building itself, the surface of each decorative object is contoured through an uninterrupted progression of planes. Subtle and elaborate details guide the eye through the linear continuities of the carved masses and the reciprocally modulated volumes. Guimard also used iconographic repetition to further unify the exterior and interior. An interlace reminiscent of Celtic manuscripts appears in the plans, and on the roof, window frames, and accessories. Earlike and slipper foot motifs, suggestive of eighteenth-century sources, are used on every piece of furniture and picture frame.

24. Study for stair hall. (ca. 1902). Green ink on tracing paper, 17 x 9¾". A.E.D.A.A.D.XX.

25. Study for stair hall. (ca. 1902). Blue ink on paper, 20½ x 15¾". A.E.D.A.A.D.XX.

26. Final elevation. 1904. Blueprint, 13½ x 19¼". Archives de Paris, Paris

27. Wall frame for a Japanese print. (ca. 1904). Gilt bronze, 21¼ x 10¾". The Museum of Modern Art, New York. Gift of Madame Hector Guimard, 1949

28. Bed with attached tablets. (ca. 1904–7). Pear wood, 63" x 7'4½" x 7'5". Musée des Arts Décoratifs, Paris. Gift of Madame Léon Nozal, 1937. *Page 18*

29. Angled cupboard. (ca. 1904–7). Pear wood, 66" high. Musée des Arts Décoratifs, Paris. Gift of Madame Léon Nozal, 1937. *Page 20*

30. Night stool. (ca. 1904–7). Pear wood, 14¾" high. Musée des Arts Décoratifs, Paris. Gift of Madame Léon Nozal, 1937. *Page 18*

31. Chaise longue. (ca. 1904–7). Pear wood without original upholstery (two pieces), 33⅛ x 67" long. Musée des Arts Décoratifs, Paris. Gift of Madame Léon Nozal, 1937. *Chair, page 26*

32. Side table with sliding tablet. (ca. 1904–7). Pear wood, 29¾" high. The Museum of Modern Art, New York. Gift of Madame Hector Guimard, 1949. *Page 18*

33. Double standing frame for photographs. (ca. 1904–7). Gilt bronze, 9½ x 14½". The Museum of Modern Art, New York. Gift of Madame Hector Guimard, 1949

34. Standing frame for a photograph. (ca. 1904–7). Fruitwood, 11⅜ x 9". Musée des Arts Décoratifs, Paris. Gift of Madame Pézieux, 1955

35. Standing frame for a photograph. 1907. Gilt bronze, 10½ x 6¾". Cooper-Hewitt Museum of Decorative Arts and Design, Smithsonian Institution, New York. Gift of Madame Hector Guimard, 1956

Façade. (Photo 1937)

LIBRARY
COLBY-SAWYER COLLEGE
NEW LONDON, NH 03257

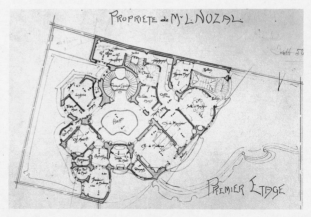

Preliminary plan. 1902. (Avery Library, Columbia University, New York)

JASSEDÉ APARTMENT HOUSE
142 avenue de Versailles, Paris
1903–5

The final architecture of the Nozal House, and the Jassedé Apartment House mark the end of Guimard's High Art Nouveau period, and the beginning of his more refined "Style Guimard" period. In place of intense chromatics appear the subtle relationships of creamy sandstone and white brick. Attention shifts from painterly qualities of animated surface to plastic qualities of contoured space.

The Jassedé Apartment House, like the later Guimard House, is a masterpiece of corner-site composition. In neither instance is there what could properly be described as one façade, or even two. Instead, a single, fluidly articulated surface smoothly turns from one plane to another. The idea is repeated in the treatment of the rounded top of the Nozal cupboard. These corner compositions are excellent examples of Guimard's ability to translate the formal quality of dynamic asymmetry—usually achieved by others only in two-dimensional and smaller, three-dimensional Art Nouveau designs—into architectural space. As with all of Guimard's buildings after about 1898, one must walk around these compositions to understand them.

Angled cupboard from Nozal House. ca. 1904–7
opposite: Detail of corner of Jassedé Apartment House

GUIMARD HOUSE
122 avenue Mozart, Paris
1909–10; outfitting 1912

After many years of being a very social bachelor, in 1909 Guimard married Adeline Oppenheim of New York. For the first time, he had the motivation and the means to lavish on his own environment the attention he had given to that of clients. During this quiet period in his professional life, Guimard devoted to his new home all the intimate concern of an artist doing a self-portrait. Thanks to the efforts of Madame Guimard, who hoped to make this house a Guimard Museum, it is the only one of his domestic interiors for which there is an almost complete photographic record.

The wrought-iron banister in the vestibule has properly been compared with both the graceful elegance of the Rococo, and the dynamic abstraction of contemporary metal sculpture. Its separate lines spring loose from their containments to overlap and intertwine with all the energy of a sensuously controlled explosion. The dining room is also an original blending of old and new ideas. The space of a Rococo oval is flooded with natural light by a complex interrelationship of wide windows, glass walls, and carefully placed mirrors. The recessed legs of the table grow naturalistically out of a mound of carpeting. Above the buffet, where most homes would have had a painting, Guimard modeled an abstract mural in the wet plaster.

Dining room. (Photo ca. 1912. Cooper-Hewitt Museum of Decorative Arts and Design, Smithsonian Institution, New York)

Perspective of corner

opposite: Stair hall. (Photo ca. 1912)

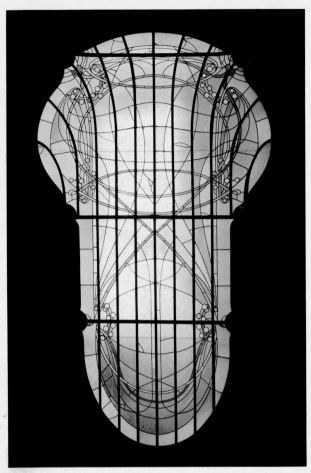

Skylight

opposite: Interior of gallery

MEZZARA HOUSE
60 rue La Fontaine, Paris
1910–11; outfitting 1912

Guimard's last interior masterpiece was the gallery of this house. Intended as an exhibition area in this combination home and workshop for a textile manufacturer, the monumental central space measures 33 feet long, 15 feet wide, and 18 feet high. The mezzanine, cantilevered on two thin columns opposite the stairway, is carried on the eight, faintly Gothic, metal ribs that support the ceiling. The climax of the room is a large stained-glass window held in the grip of the metal ribs like a jewel in a medieval crown. Above it, natural light falls uninterruptedly through a broad, three-story opening in the center of the building and cascades into the gallery through the filtering membrane. As with all of Guimard's spaces, the manner in which the light is permitted to enter is controlled as carefully as is each tangible material, and plays a principal role in the overall psychological effect.

Although a very late design, marking a transition into the geometry of Art Déco, the window composition still contains the dual qualities characteristic of his High Art Nouveau style—the gentleness of pastel coloring and linear strength as dynamic as Henri Bergson's *élan vital*.

CHAIRS

"When I design a piece of furniture or sculpt it, I reflect upon the spectacle the universe provides. Beauty appears to us in a perpetual variety. No parallelism or symmetry: forms are engendered from movements which are never alike . . . And what a lesson for the architect, for the artist who knows how to look at this wonderful repertoire of forms and colors! For construction, do not the branches of the trees, the stems, by turn rigid and undulating, furnish us with models? You will tell me that if I apply the example of the stem's movements, and the disparities within these movements, to furniture, to everyday objects . . . I will end up with the effect of cut-outs. Inaccurate! You only have this impression because you are accustomed to furniture conceived as antique monuments. These dominant lines which describe space, sometimes supple and sinuous arabesques, sometimes flourishes as vivid as the firing of a thunderbolt, these lines have a value of feeling and expression more eloquent than the vertical, horizontal and regular lines continually used until now in architecture . . . Let us be inspired by these general laws. Let us bend before . . . the examples of the great architect of the universe." (Guimard to Victor Champier, *Revue des Arts Décoratifs*, 1899)

36. Side chair. (ca. 1899). Fruitwood without original upholstery, 38⅛″ high. Private collection, Paris

37. Armchair. (ca. 1899). Fruitwood without original upholstery, 41¾″ high. Private collection, Paris. *Page 27*

38. Armchair. (ca. 1899–1900). Walnut and tooled leather; 32½″ high. The Museum of Modern Art, New York. Gift of Madame Hector Guimard, 1949

39. Study for an armchair. (ca. 1899–1901). Crayon and pencil on paper, 40 x 25½″. A.E.D.A.A.D.XX.

40. Study for an armchair. (ca. 1899–1901). Crayon, pastel, and pencil on paper, 45⅝ x 26″. A.E.D.A.A.D.XX.

41. Studies for a side chair. (ca. 1899–1901). Crayon, pastel, and pencil on paper, 34 x 58″. A.E.D.A.A.D.XX.

42. Study for a side chair. (ca. 1901–3). Crayon, pastel, and pencil on paper, 42½ x 30¾″. A.E.D.A.A.D.XX.

43. Studies for a side chair. (ca. 1901–3). Crayon, pastel, and pencil on paper, 50⅜ x 32¾″. A.E.D.A.A.D.XX.

44. Side chair. (ca. 1902–3). Fruitwood and tooled leather, 42½″ high. Private collection, Paris

45. Armchair. (ca. 1902–3). Fruitwood and tooled leather, 41¾″ high. Private collection, Paris

46. Study for side chair. (ca. 1902–7). Pencil and watercolor on tracing paper, 43 x 25¼″. A.E.D.A.A.D.XX.

47. Side chair. (ca. 1904–7). Cherry and plush upholstery, 43½″ high. The Museum of Modern Art, New York. Gift of Madame Hector Guimard, 1949

48. Side chair. (ca. 1909–12). Cherry and tooled leather, 44″ high. Musée d'Art Moderne de la Ville de Paris. Gift of Madame Hector Guimard, 1948

49. Armchair. (ca. 1909–12). Cherry and leather, 43⅝″ high. Philadelphia Museum of Art. Gift of Madame Hector Guimard, 1948.*

Armchair. ca. 1899

opposite: Armchair from Nozal House. ca. 1904–7. Part of chaise longue

GRAPHICS

Inspired by medieval art as well as Japanese and Belgian sources, Guimard achieved his first fully mature Art Nouveau designs in 1896 while making wainscoting and wallpapers. The same highly animated linearity infused his original lettering and treatment of the printed page. His interest in graphic design was primarily limited to covers and title pages, seldom extending to the typography and layout of entire books. Very few examples of Guimard's printed designs survive. The largest body of evidence for his imaginative lettering is the sketches and working drawings, in which the graphics are an integral part of the overall composition.

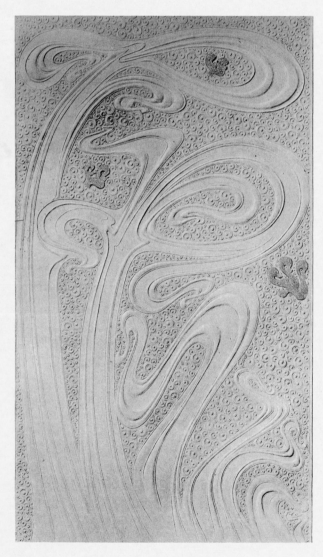

Lincrusta. 1896

50. Study for lincrusta. (1896). Pencil and crayon on paper, 21⅜ x 28⅛". A.E.D.A.A.D.XX.

51. Lincrusta. (1896). Pressed *papier mâché*, 39 x 23⅝". Private collection, Paris. *Page 28*

52. Wallpaper for anterooms. (1896). Stenciled paint, 40⅛ x 19⅝". Bibliothèque Forney, Paris

53. Wallpaper for bedrooms. (1896). Stenciled paint, 32⅝ x 19⅝". Bibliothèque Forney, Paris

54. Wallpaper for dining rooms. (1896). Stenciled paint, 29½ x 19⅝". Bibliothèque Forney, Paris

55. Wallpaper for living rooms. (1896; facsimile 1970). Silkscreen, 27⅛" wide. Courtesy Larsen Design Studio, New York. *Cover*

56. Wallpaper. (ca. 1896). Stenciled paint, 38½ x 19⅝". Bibliothèque Forney, Paris

57. Cover of portfolio: *Le Castel Béranger*. 1898. Green fiberboard stamped with gold leaf, 13 x 17⅜". The Museum of Modern Art, New York. Gift of Lillian Nassau, 1967

58. Title page of portfolio: *Le Castel Béranger*. (1898). Lithograph and letterpress, 12½ x 17". The Museum of Modern Art, New York. Gift of Lillian Nassau, 1967. *Page 29*

59. Invitation: *Exposition/Salon du Figaro/Le Castel Béranger*. (1899). Letterpress, 4½ x 6⅝". Private collection, Paris

60. Poster: *Exposition/Salon du Figaro/Le Castel Béranger*. (1889). Lithograph, 35 x 49¼". The Museum of Modern Art, New York. Gift of Lillian Nassau, 1968

61. Study for magazine cover: *Revue d'Art*. (1899). Pencil, ink, and watercolor on tracing paper, 16¾ x 11⅛". A.E.D.A.A.D.XX.

62. Magazine cover: *Revue d'Art No. 7*. 1899. Letterpress, 12 x 8". The Museum of Modern Art, New York. Promised gift of Stan Ries

63. Five studies for plaster friezes. 1902. Watercolor, matted 24 x 19⅛". Bibliothèque des Arts Décoratifs, Paris. Gift of Madame Hector Guimard, 1948

64. Invitation: *Exposition de l'Habitation*. 1903. Letterpress, 3½" x 5⅜". Bibliothèque des Arts Décoratifs, Paris

65. Portfolio of postcards: *Exposition de l'Habitation*. 1903. Letterpress, 5½ x 3½". The Museum of Modern Art, New York. Gift of Madame Hector Guimard, 1949

66. Cover of catalogue: *Fontes Artistiques*. 1907. Gray paper stamped with silver leaf, 10¾ x 14¾". Private collection, Paris

Title page of portfolio: Le Castel Béranger. *1898*

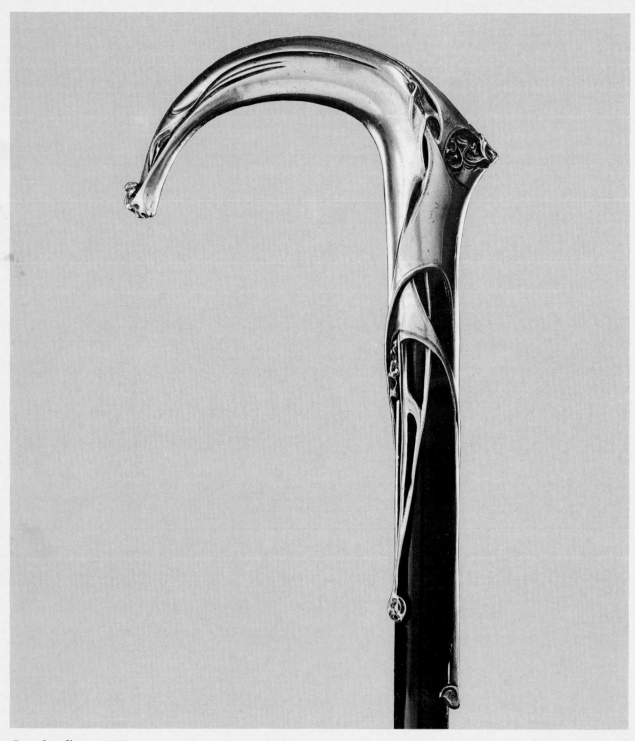

Cane handle. ca. 1909

PERSONAL ACCESSORIES

Few objects for personal use are known from Guimard's early career. His desire to design such pieces developed shortly before his marriage in 1909 for which he designed his bride's ring and wedding gown, if not also his magnificent cane. Their new home was the setting for most, if not all, of the surviving textiles. They range from fluid linearity to the more crisp ovals and interlaces, which are indicative of the transition from Art Nouveau to Art Déco.

Less personal but equally individual are the cologne bottles produced industrially for the Paris Exposition of 1900. They were signed in the mold with the monogram "HG," as were his early vases.

67. Cologne bottle. (1900). Clear cast glass and printed label, 7¾" high. Parfums Revillon—F. Millot, Paris. *Page 31*

68. Cologne bottle. (1900). Clear cast glass and printed label, 11" high. Parfums Revillon—F. Millot, Paris

69. Cologne bottle. (1900). Clear cast glass, 15" high. Martin J. Eidelburg, New Brunswick, New Jersey

70. Letter opener. 1907. Rosewood, 6¾" long. The Museum of Modern Art, New York. Gift of Madame Hector Guimard, 1949

71. Tray. 1907. Rosewood, 19¾" long. The Museum of Modern Art, New York. Gift of Madame Hector Guimard

72. Seal. (ca. 1908). Gilt bronze, 3½" high. Laurent Oppenheim, Jr., New York

73. Hatpin. (ca. 1908). Bronze without original stones, 1¼" diameter. The Museum of Modern Art, New York. Gift of Madame Hector Guimard, 1949

74. Platter. 1909. Gilt bronze, 18¼" diameter. Musée des Arts Décoratifs, Paris. Purchase, 1911

75. Umbrella handle. 1909. Bronze and ivory, 9¼" long. The Museum of Modern Art, New York. Promised gift of Mr. and Mrs. Alfred H. Barr, Jr.

76. Cane handle. (ca. 1909). Silver, 8" long. Private collection, Paris. *Page 30*

77. Panel for wedding gown of Adeline Oppenheim (Madame Guimard). (1909). Embroidered silk, 45¼ x 15⅜". Cooper-Hewitt Museum of Decorative Arts and Design, Smithsonian Institution, New York. Gift of Madame Hector Guimard, 1949.*

78. Study for embroidery. (ca. 1909–12). Embroidered silk and pencil, 26¾ x 11⅜". Cooper-Hewitt Museum of Decorative Arts and Design, Smithsonian Institution, New York. Gift of Madame Hector Guimard, 1949.*

79. Tea cloth. (ca. 1909–12). Embroidered linen, 23⅝ x 22⅜". Cooper-Hewitt Museum of Decorative Arts and Design, Smithsonian Institution, New York. Gift of Madame Hector Guimard, 1949.*

80. Study for a window curtain. (ca. 1909–12). Embroidered silk and paint, 24 x 13½". The Metropolitan Museum of Art, New York. Gift of Madame Hector Guimard, 1949.*

81. Window curtain. (ca. 1909–12). Embroidered silk, 6'3" x 17". The Metropolitan Museum of Art, New York. Gift of Madame Hector Guimard, 1949.*

Cologne bottle. 1900

Planter. 1899–1900

Vase. 1899–1900

opposite: Vase. ca. 1898

VASES

The earliest known vases, designed by 1898, all seem to have been for Guimard's own use. The Sèvres ceramics of 1900 and 1903 may have been executed in somewhat larger editions. By about 1907, he had decided to execute his models industrially in both cast iron and ceramic. Some of these mass-produced pieces are of a quality comparable to the finest handmade designs.

These vases are excellent examples of his empathetic approach to materials. The formal characteristics of the design suggest the intrinsic properties of the material, whether the articulations are short and thick for the limited structural properties of ceramic, or long and thin and fluid for molten bronze or cast iron.

82. Vase. (ca. 1898). Bronze, 10½″ high. Henri Poupée, Paris. *Page 33*

83. Vase. (1899–1900). Glazed porcelain, 10¾″ high. Cooper-Hewitt Museum of Decorative Arts and Design, Smithsonian Institution, New York. Gift of Madame Hector Guimard, 1948. *Page 32*

84. Planter. (1899–1900). Glazed porcelain, 11″ high. Gerhard P. Woeckel, Munich. *Page 32*

85. Vase (ca. 1905–7). Gilt bronze, 10½″ high. Cooper-Hewitt Museum of Decorative Arts and Design, Smithsonian Institution, New York. Gift of Madame Hector Guimard, 1956

86. Planter and stand. (1907). Cast iron, painted with gold (two pieces), 56¾″ high. Private collection, Paris

87. Planter. (1907). Cast iron, 20½″ high. Alastair B. Martin, New York

ARCHITECTURAL ACCESSORIES

Guimard always devoted particular attention to the first objects one touched on entering one of his houses—the doorbells and doorknobs. But he was no less interested in bestowing on something as humble as a nail cover an elegance usually reserved for jewelry. Most of the early accessories were done in limited editions for particular buildings. Guimard gradually realized that the machine could be used as effectively as any other tool, and that the quality of an industrially produced object could be as high as that of a handmade object, as long as one could learn to control the production process.

Before 1900 he had begun to repeat individual designs; during and after 1900 he also designed vases, textiles, lighting fixtures, and furniture for industrial production. The most successful of these commercial ventures was a large series of cast-iron architectural accessories and furniture that was manufactured as *Fontes Artistiques* from 1907 until 1937.

88.   Stair-rod pin. (ca. 1896). Brass, 2″ high. Private collection, San Francisco

89.   Doorknob. (ca. 1896). Brass, 3⅞″ wide. Barlach Heuer, Paris

90.   Doorknob. (By 1898). White porcelain, 2⅞″ wide. John Jesse, London

91.   Doorknob. (By 1898). Blue porcelain, 2⅞″ wide. Private collection, Paris

92.   Study for radiator grill. (ca. 1900). Watercolor and pencil on tracing paper. 21¼ x 19″. A.E.D.A.A.D.XX. *Page 34*

93.   Doorbell cover. (ca. 1902–7). Bronze, 3¼″ wide. Lillian Nassau, New York

94.   Umbrella stand. (Before 1907). Cast iron, painted, 33″ high. The Museum of Modern Art, New York. Gift of Madame Hector Guimard, 1949

95.   Numerals "52". (ca. 1905–7). Cast iron, recently painted, 8⅝ x 12⅛″. Private collection, Paris

96.   Balcony railing. (ca. 1905–7). Cast iron, painted, 40 x 63¾″. The Museum of Modern Art, New York. Gift of Phyllis B. Lambert, 1960

97.   Fireplace. (ca. 1907). Cast iron, painted white, 35½ x 33½″. Lillian Nassau, New York

98.   Curtain-rod finials. (ca. 1907). Metal, recently gilt, each 8½″ long. Private collection, Paris

99.   Nail cover. (ca. 1909–12). Gilt bronze, 1⅝″ diameter. Private collection, Paris. *Page 35*

100.   Doorbell pull. (ca. 1909–12). Gilt bronze, 7⅞″ high. Cooper-Hewitt Museum of Decorative Arts and Design, Smithsonian Institution, New York. Gift of Madame Hector Guimard, 1948

101.   Door handle. (ca. 1909–12). Gilt bronze, 4¾″ high. The Museum of Modern Art, New York. Gift of Madame Hector Guimard, 1949

102.   Key to buffet. (ca. 1909–12). Silver-plated metal, 2¾″ long. Musée d'Art Moderne de la Ville de Paris. Gift of Madame Hector Guimard, 1948

103.   Drawer pull. (ca. 1913). Silver-plated metal, 4⅜″ long. Philadelphia Museum of Art. Gift of Madame Hector Guimard, 1948

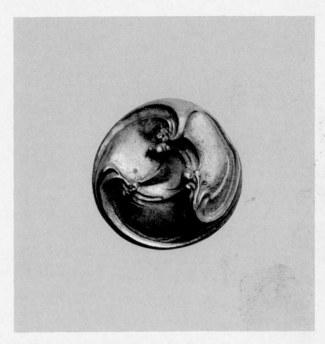

Nail cover. ca. 1909–12

opposite: Study for radiator grill. ca. 1900

TRUSTEES OF PARTICIPATING MUSEUMS

The Museum of Modern Art, New York

David Rockefeller, *Chairman*; Henry Allen Moe, John Hay Whitney, and Gardner Cowles, *Vice Chairmen*; William S. Paley, *President*; James Thrall Soby and Mrs. Bliss Parkinson, *Vice Presidents*; Willard C. Butcher, *Treasurer*; Walter Bareiss, Robert R. Barker, Alfred H. Barr, Jr.*, William A. M. Burden, J. Frederic Byers III, Ivan Chermayeff, Mrs. W. Murray Crane*, John de Menil, Mrs. C. Douglas Dillon, Mrs. Edsel B. Ford, George Heard Hamilton, Wallace K. Harrison*, Mrs. Walter Hochschild*, James W. Husted*, Philip Johnson, Mrs. Frank Y. Larkin, Mrs. Albert D. Lasker, John L. Loeb, Ranald H. Macdonald*, Mrs. G. Macculloch Miller*, Mrs. Charles S. Payson, Gifford Phillips, Mrs. John D. Rockefeller 3rd, Nelson A. Rockefeller, Mrs. Wolfgang Schoenborn, Mrs. Bertram Smith, Mrs. Donald B. Straus, Walter N. Thayer, Edward M. M. Warburg*, Monroe Wheeler*.
* Honorary Trustee for Life

California Palace of the Legion of Honor, San Francisco

William R. Wallace, *President*; Mrs. Alexander Albert, Louis A. Benoist, Joseph M. Bransten, Charles C. de Limur, R. Stanley Dollar, Jr., Mrs. Frederick J. Hellman, Mrs. Robert Homans, Mrs. Bruce Kelham, Walter S. Newman, William L. Olds, David Pleydell-Bouverie, Whitney Warren, Harold L. Zellerbach; *Ex Officio*: The Honorable Joseph L. Alioto, Walter H. Shorenstein.

Art Gallery of Ontario, Toronto

Edmund C. Bovey, *President*; J. Douglas Crashley, John H. Devlin, John H. Moore, F.C.A., and Robert N. Steiner, *Vice Presidents*; Mrs. Thomas J. Bata, Edgar G. Burton, Mrs. Margaret Campbell, Q.C., William A. Cowan, Q.C., James S. Craig, M.R.I.A.C., Mrs. Harry Davidson, Frederik S. Eaton, Mrs. John D. Eaton, George R. Gardiner, Marvin B. Gelber, George W. Gilmour, Henry R. Jackman, Q.C., Patrick T. Johnson, Mrs. Oscar Kofman, John B. Ridley, Mrs. Elizabeth A. Stevens, Richard M. Thomson, Gordon D. Tiller, Samuel J. Zacks.

NA 1053 .G8 G7 c.1
Graham, F. Lanier.
Hector Guimard

DATE DUE	

GAYLORD   PRINTED IN U.S.A.